Produced for A & C Black by
Monkey Puzzle Media Ltd
11 Chanctonbury Road
Hove BN3 6EL, UK

Published by A & C Black Publishers
Limited, 36 Soho Square
London W1D 3QY

First published 2011

www.acblack.com

ISBN HB 978-1-4081-4039-0
      PB 978-1-4081-4038-3

A CIP catalogue record for this book is
available from the British Library.

Editor: Dan Rogers
Design: Mayer Media
Picture research: Lynda Lines

Picture acknowledgements
Alamy pp. 1 (Steve Bly), 6 (Aurora
Photos), 8 (Peter Brown), 9 (David
Moore), 10 (Aurora Photos), 14 (Philip
Quirk), 16 (Rob Watkins), 17 (Chris
Cheadle), 18 (Ryan Bonneau), 19
(Ryan Bonneau), 20 (Stock Connection
Distribution), 21 (Steve Bly), 22 (RJH
Catalog), 25 (Larry Larsen); Corbis
p. 11 (AlaskaStock); Louisiana Office
of Tourism pp. 12, 13; MPM Images
p. 28; Nature Picture Library p. 29
(Jeff Vanuga); Photolibrary pp. 5 (Aflo
Foto Agency), 23 (All Canada Photos);
Rex Features pp. 4 (Hot Stock), 15
(Ian Bird), 24; Wikimedia pp. 7, 26;
Zice Holidays p. 27. Compass rose
artwork on front cover and inside
pages by iStockphoto. Map artwork
by MPM Images.

The front cover shows a fly fisherman
catching a trout in Colorado, USA
(Photolibrary/Hot Stock).

Every effort has been made to
contact copyright holders of material
reproduced in this book. Any omissions
will be rectified in subsequent printings
if notice is given to the publishers.

SAFETY ADVICE

Don't attempt any of the
activities or techniques
in this book without the
guidance of a qualified
instructor or guide.

WORLD: Fishing

Paul Mason

A&C Black • London

CONTENTS

It's a Fish-Filled World

You're slowly winding in the reel and suddenly there's a tug
on your fishing rod. The line starts to zip outwards – a fish!
And a big one, by the feel of it. But what exactly is on the
end of your line? You'll only find out by using all your skill
and reeling in the fish without losing it.

A bass fights to free itself from an angler's line.
Once it had been reeled in, this fish
was released back into the wild.

THE SECRET LANGUAGE OF FISHING

lures artificial baits, made of
plastic or metal
breakable able to be pulled
apart into smaller pieces

THE WORLD OF FISHING

You can go fishing practically anywhere you find water. People fish in freezing Arctic seas, warm Indian lakes, fast-flowing rivers in the Rockies, Andes and Alps, and every one of the world's seas and oceans. They have developed all kinds of different fishing gear, too. (If it seems confusing, don't worry! There is plenty of advice on equipment in this book.)

THE WORLD'S BEST FISHING SPOTS

Imagine you could go fishing anywhere in the world. Where would you go? Where are the absolute BEST places to fish? This book will tell you what you need to know, so just turn the page to find out more.

Ideal fishing kit for a beginner. A rod and reel like these can be used for both float fishing and spinning.

Technical: Fishing equipment

There are thousands of different combinations of rods, reels, lines and tackle that you can use for fishing. These are the main different kinds:

River fishing:

• Many people use a "float rod", a light rod about 3 metres (10 feet) long.

• The most common reel is a fixed-spool reel.

• Thin nylon line, and a variety of floats, hooks and baits, depending on what you want to catch.

Sea fishing:

• Beach-casting rods are usually about 4 metres (13 feet) long. Boat-fishing rods are shorter, and more sturdy.

• Fixed-spool reels are most common.

• Thin nylon line, and a variety of hooks, baits and **lures**.

Sport and game fishing:

• Fly-fishing or spinning rods are light and usually about 2.75 metres (9 feet) long.

• Fixed-spool reels for spinning; special fly reels for fly-fishing.

• Thin nylon line and spinning lures for spinning; thicker lines and flies for fly fishing.

For a beginner, the best fishing kit is probably a fixed-spool reel, a light, **breakable** rod about 2.75 metres (9 feet) long, and a variety of lures and floats.

River Arno

RIVER ARNO
Location: Florence, Italy
Type of fishing: river (bank)
Difficulty level: 1 of 5
Best season: May to June and September to October

Just to prove that you can find great fishing almost anywhere, our first stop is in the middle of the ancient city of Florence, Italy. Here you can cast a line into the river, as the bells of the thousand-year-old church towers ring out in the morning.

Tip from a Local

The giant catfish caught in the Arno in 2007 (see opposite) was hooked using a bait of old bread.

SKILL
Tying a hook or weight to the end of a line

You'll never catch a fish unless your hook is tied on securely! This is a simple, reliable way to tie a hook or weight to the end of a fishing line:

1. Thread the line through the eye of the hook/weight, then make a loop on the end of the line.

2. Turn the end of the line over the section of line leading from the tip of the rod to the hook/weight, and back through the loop. Repeat five or six times.

3. Pull the line tight. Take care not to catch your fingers or thumb on the tip of the hook – it's easily done!

4. Just before it's really tight, wet the knot with spit or water. Then pull it tight. You're now ready to hook a fish!

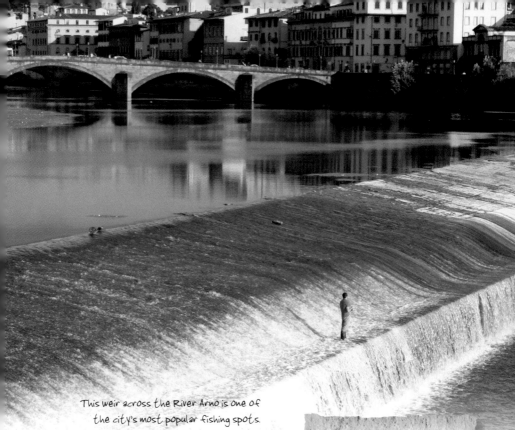

This weir across the River Arno is one of the city's most popular fishing spots.

THE SECRET LANGUAGE OF FISHING

tackle shop shop selling fishing equipment

If you like the River Arno...
... you could also try:
• River Aire, Leeds, England
• Hudson River, New York, USA

FISHING THE RIVER ARNO
The best fishing spots are right in the city centre, downstream from the market. Legends tell of a giant fish that stalks the Arno, and in 2007 a huge catfish weighing 30 kilograms (66 pounds) and 1.7 metres (5.6 feet) long was caught. The fish was released back into the river, and it's still there, waiting to be caught again.

ESSENTIAL INFORMATION
Fishing is best here in the spring and autumn. Fish for catfish, goldfish and crucian carp.

Fishing equipment: Simple reel and breakable rod. Ask in local **tackle shops** for bait.

Clothing: In spring, summer and autumn, light clothing is fine (with a jacket if necessary). Winters can be cold, especially by the river.

Dungeness Beach

DUNGENESS BEACH
Location: Kent, England
Type of fishing: sea (beach)
Difficulty level: 1.5 of 5
Best season: September to January

At first sight, Dungeness might not seem like a very attractive place to fish. It's a flat, gloomy **spit** of shingle that sticks out into the English Channel. Worse, there's a nuclear power station perched on the end of it. So why come here? Because you might catch some BIG fish!

FISHING DUNGENESS BEACH

Dungeness is one of the few places where you can still catch big cod from the beach. Cod of over 10 kilograms (22 pounds) are occasionally reeled in. But you might find almost anything on the end of your line here, including sea bass, whiting and all kinds of flatfish.

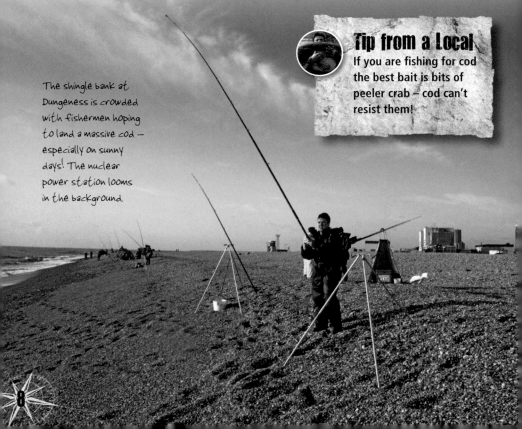

Tip from a Local
If you are fishing for cod the best bait is bits of peeler crab – cod can't resist them!

The shingle bank at Dungeness is crowded with fishermen hoping to land a massive cod – especially on sunny days! The nuclear power station looms in the background.

THE SECRET LANGUAGE OF FISHING

spit narrow piece of land sticking out into the sea

live bait bait of living (or recently dead) animals, such as worms

ESSENTIAL INFORMATION

Early autumn is a good time to visit Dungeness. You have a chance of good weather (or at least not freezing weather), and all kinds of fish will be biting.

Fishing equipment: For cod, a beach-casting rod that can make long casts. For bass, the biggest fish are usually within about 15 metres (50 feet) of the shore. **Live bait** is best.

Clothing: It can get chilly, so always make sure you've got a warm jacket, hat and gloves.

If you like Dungeness Beach...

... you could also try:
• Orford Ness, England
• Skarnsundet Fjordsenter, Norway
• Cape Cod, Massachusetts, USA

SKILL
Beach casting

The rod whips through as this angler makes a long, two-handed cast from the beach.

When fishing from a beach, you may have to cast a long way out. Here's a technique to try (these instructions are for someone right-handed, so reverse them if you're left-handed):

1. Grip the rod with both hands, turn to the right, and point your left shoulder where you want to cast. Swing the rod backwards until it is pointing behind you, and the weight is lying on the ground.

2. Turn your head to look where you want to cast, then firmly and smoothly pull the rod up and forwards. Twist your body around to the left, like a baseball hitter, as you cast.

3. Pull down with your left arm and push forward with your right, to add power to the cast.

Experts can cast over 100 metres (330 feet) with a cast like this – which gets their bait into very deep water!

Fort Peck Lake

You couldn't make a list of the world's best places to fish without including Montana. Expert fly fishermen head here to fish in the fast-flowing rivers. But for a beginner, Fort Peck Lake is a perfect place to try spinning for all kinds of fish.

FORT PECK LAKE
Location: Montana, USA
Type of fishing: lake (boat)
Difficulty level: 2 of 5
Best season: May to September for trout

If you like Fort Peck Lake...

... you could also try:
- Lake Nasser, Egypt
- Loch Katrine, Scotland

FISHING FORT PECK LAKE

There are more than 50 different species of fish swimming about in Fort Peck Lake. They include walleye, northern pike, salmon, smallmouth bass and trout. Of these, trout is one of the most exciting to catch. Trout fight hard when hooked, and anglers need skill and patience to reel them in.

Montana's rivers and beautiful landscapes make it a must-visit destination for anglers. This young girl has caught a trout using fly-fishing gear.

Tip from a Local
If you really can't bear to be away from the fishing for long, try staying on a houseboat – there are several moored on the lake!

Smile for the camera! He probably doesn't feel much like smiling, but this trout is about to be released back into the river, which should cheer him up.

SKILL
Landing a fish

ESSENTIAL INFORMATION

Since the lake is 216 kilometres (134 miles) long, and steep-sided in places, the best fishing is from a boat. Be careful not to hook your fellow sailors when casting!

Fishing equipment: A standard 2.75-metre (9-foot) spinning rod, a fixed-spool reel containing 3.5-kilogram (7.7-pound) **breaking strain** line, and a selection of spinning lures.

Clothing: Dress for the season but always be aware that storms can develop suddenly on the lake.

THE SECRET LANGUAGE OF FISHING

breaking strain weight that will break a fishing line

lip grippers soft pincers used for gripping a fish's mouth

Once you have caught a fish, you need to "land" it – bring it safely to shore and remove the hook from its mouth.

1. Once there is only as much line out as the length of your rod, stop reeling in. So, for a 2.75-metre (9-foot) rod, stop reeling when there are 2.75 metres (9 feet) of line stretching from the tip of the rod.

2. Lift the rod into the air, which will guide the fish towards you. Be ready to let out some line if it makes a last-gasp escape attempt!

3. Guide the fish into your landing net, and put down the rod. Grip the fish firmly but not too hard, ideally with a pair of **lip grippers**.

4. Remove the hook. You might need to use a degorger (a special blunt blade with a notched tip) if the hook is deep inside the fish.

Grand Isle Tarpon Rodeo

The Grand Isle Tarpon Rodeo is the oldest fishing contest in the USA. It began in 1928, and today has become one of the biggest, most fun fishing events anywhere. The fishing contest is combined with a music festival, and the usual Grand Isle population of about 1500 people grows to 20 000 or so.

GRAND ISLE TARPON RODEO
Location: Louisiana, USA
Type of fishing: sea (boat)
Difficulty level: 2.5 of 5
Held: July

The weigh-in at the end of a day's fishing during the Grand Isle Tarpon Rodeo.

TARPON FISHING

Tarpon is one of the greatest saltwater **game fish**. It is also called the Silver King. The most exciting ways to catch tarpon are fly fishing and spinning. It is tricky to **set** a hook in a tarpon's mouth, which is so hard that some anglers say it is like concrete. Tarpon are incredibly strong and, once hooked, can sometimes fight for hours to escape.

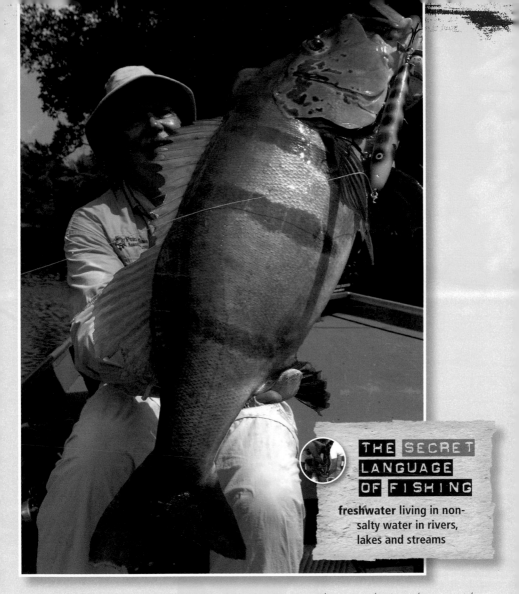

This angler in Brazil has hauled in a whopper of a peacock bass. This must be one of the largest ever caught.

THAI GIANT STINGRAY

These giants are found in just a few rivers in Southeast Asia and northern Australia. A 256-kilogram (563-pound) giant stingray was caught in Thailand using a rod and line – the biggest fish ever to be caught that way. It was then released back into the wild.

"CHOY'S MONSTER"

In 1970, a group of anglers off Oahu, Hawaii, landed the largest blue marlin ever caught with a rod and line. It weighed 818.7 kilograms (1805 pounds) and was named "Choy's Monster" after Cornelius Choy, the skipper of the fishing boat.

Himalaya Mountains

The Himalayas are the world's highest mountains. In spring, melting snow turns to water, and comes rushing down from the peaks. The rivers fill with fast-flowing water, crashing its way to the plains thousands of metres below. What a great place to fish!

FISHING INDIA'S HIMALAYAS

Fast-flowing rivers like these breed strong fish. Strongest of all is your prey – the golden mahseer. Many anglers say this is the most aggressive fish they have ever hooked. The largest mahseer ever caught weighed 55 kilograms (121 pounds). That was many years ago. Today, the effects of overfishing and poaching mean that none of the largest fish survive.

HIMALAYA MOUNTAINS
Location: India
Type of fishing: river (bank)
Difficulty level: 4.5 of 5
Best season: March to October, but not during **monsoon** season

The lakes and fast-flowing rivers of the Himalayas are home to strong, hard-fighting fish. Catching them is a real challenge, even for expert anglers.

Tip from a Local
Bring some sturdy walking boots – it can be a long hike to reach the fishing spots!

If you like the Himalayas...
... you could also try:
• The Rockies, North America
• The Andes, South America

THE SECRET LANGUAGE OF FISHING

monsoon period of very heavy rain in South Asia

fishery area where fish can be caught

Not many anglers can say they have caught a golden mahseer like this one. These fish are increasingly rare, and most anglers return them to the water after landing them.

ESSENTIAL INFORMATION

The best time to fish for mahseer is before or after the monsoon. During the monsoon itself, **fisheries** are closed.

Fishing equipment: The most exciting way to catch mahseer is by fly fishing or spinning; take equipment that can cope with heavy fish. You will also need a pair of waders.

Clothing: Long-sleeved shirt and trousers, hat and sunscreen.

Information: Conserving fish stocks

Many of the world's most popular fish, including the golden mahseer, are becoming endangered. Unless something is done, they may soon die out completely. The mahseer is a good example of what anglers can do to help stop the fall in fish numbers.

• Only ever take a mahseer's picture home with you, not the actual fish. Once caught, it should be released back into the river.

• Do not fish during the monsoon: mahseer fisheries are closed because the fish are laying their eggs at this time.

• Once you have caught a golden mahseer, stop fishing. You have already become one of a tiny number of the world's anglers to reel one in. Why be greedy?

Rio Palena

By this stage of your fishing journey around the world, you'll be an expert in just about every kind of fishing. It's time to head for northern Patagonia. Here you'll be rubbing shoulders with Hollywood stars and ex-presidents, in some of the world's most amazing fly-fishing spots.

RIO PALENA
Location: northern Patagonia, Chile
Type of fishing: river (bank or boat)
Difficulty level: 4.5 of 5
Best season: November to March

FISHING RIO PALENA

The waters of Rio Palena come washing down from the **glaciers** in the mountains above. Clean and fast, they are perfect for trout (which were imported to the region in the 1800s). Northern Patagonia is very isolated: few anglers come here and the rivers are full of fish. Most anglers want to keep things that way, so they use catch-and-release techniques.

THE SECRET LANGUAGE OF FISHING

glacier large, slow-moving "river" of ice and squashed-down snow at the top of a mountain valley

ESSENTIAL INFORMATION

The best season to visit is high summer – during the winter (between June and August) the best fishing spots are snowed in and cannot be reached.

Fishing equipment: A standard 2.75-metre (9-foot) fly rod and medium-weight line will be perfect.

Clothing: Summer days are warm, but this high up the sun is very strong. Cover your skin and wear sunblock. Mountain weather can change fast, so always take a rain jacket and a warm layer.

Tip from a Local

For a change from fishing, visit a rodeo one evening – most towns hold them twice a month during the summer.

Almost anywhere else in the world, there would probably be a crowd of anglers at a great fishing location like this. In Patagonia, you can fish rivers like this one on your own, if you want to.

If you like Rio Palena...

... you could also try:
• The Falkland Islands, UK Overseas Territory
• Fiordland National Park, New Zealand

SKILL
Fishing safety on big, fast-flowing rivers

Rio Palena can be a dangerous place to fish – like many great trout rivers in the mountains. The waters are fast-flowing and powerful, so anglers who wade in need to be very careful not to be swept away.

Wearing the right gear will make fishing in fast-flowing water safer and more fun.

• Always wear a flotation vest, ideally one that will self-inflate if you fall into the water.

• Never wade into water where you cannot see the bottom. Murky water can hide holes, slippery rocks, and other hazards that could trip you.

• Carry a mobile phone in a sealed waterproof bag. That way, if the worst happens, at least you'll be able to call for help!

Glossary

WORDS FROM THE SECRET LANGUAGE FEATURES

barb backwards-facing spine at the tip of a hook. Barbs can be taken away by filing them off, or crushing them flat with a pair of pliers.

breakable able to be pulled apart into smaller pieces. Most fishing rods break into between two and seven pieces, for easy transport.

breaking strain weight that will break a fishing line

fishery area where fish can be caught

freshwater living in non-salty water in rivers, lakes and streams

game fish fish that fight hard to escape when hooked

glacier large, slow-moving "river" of ice and squashed-down snow at the top of a mountain valley

lagoon large area of shallow water

lip grippers soft pincers used for gripping a fish's mouth

live bait bait of living (or recently dead) animals, such as worms

loch Scottish lake; in Ireland, known as a lough

lures artificial baits, made of plastic or metal

monsoon period of very heavy rain in South Asia

set snag or catch your hook in the fish's mouth

skiff small, wide boat that can float in very shallow water

spit narrow piece of land sticking out into the sea

tackle shop shop selling fishing equipment

trace length of wire or strong nylon leading from the end of the fishing line to the hook

turning tide time when the tide changes direction

OTHER WORDS ANGLERS USE

bivvy domed tent with a large opening at the front, for shelter while night fishing

coarse fish all freshwater fish apart from trout and salmon

deadbait bait that is dead

forceps long, thin pliers that can be used to remove a hook from a fish's mouth

match fishing competitive form of coarse fishing

pole fishing fishing using a pole and line, but no reel

quiver tip rod with a very bendy tip, which bends when a fish nibbles on the bait

Finding Out More

THE INTERNET

www.fishing.co.uk
A British fishing site, but with information about fishing around the world. Want to know what the fishing's like in Namibia, the British record sizes for a variety of fish types or just where you'd be able to fish for zander? The answers are here.

www.environment-agency.gov.uk
Click on "At home and leisure", then "Fishing" in the Outdoor Recreation category. You'll find information about where to go fishing, advice on protecting the environment, and where to go to get a rod licence (which everyone over the age of 12 must have to fish in fresh water in the UK).

www.sea-fishing.org/nfsa-size-limits. html
Important information on how large sea fish of different types have to be before you can keep them. Any smaller than the sizes listed, and you have to return them to the sea.

BOOKS FOR YOUNGER READERS

Recreational Sports: Fishing Paul Mason (Macmillan Library, 2008)

Get Outdoors: Fishing Nick Ross (Wayland, 2008)

Both of these books contain basic information for young readers about fishing, including useful equipment and techniques.

OTHER BOOKS

The New Complete Guide to Fishing Skills Tony Whieldon (Cassell Illustrated, 2007)
This book is aimed at adults as well as children, but is very clear and easy to understand, with lots of explanatory diagrams. It goes into detail about equipment and techniques for fishing on rivers and lakes or the sea, plus fly fishing and the kinds of fish you might aim to catch.

MAGAZINES

Most fishing magazines carry a mixture of articles on equipment, personalities, contests and travel. They all have websites you can locate by searching by name.

Total Fishing (for all kinds of fishing), *Fly Fishing and Fly Tying* and *Total Sea Fishing*
These UK-based magazines carry travel articles, features and equipment reviews, mostly on British and European fishing.

Fly Fisherman and *Bassmaster*
These magazines are focused mainly on fishing in North America.

Modern Fishing and *Fishing World*
These high-quality Australian magazines give a taste of fishing in one of the world's best countries for anglers.

Index

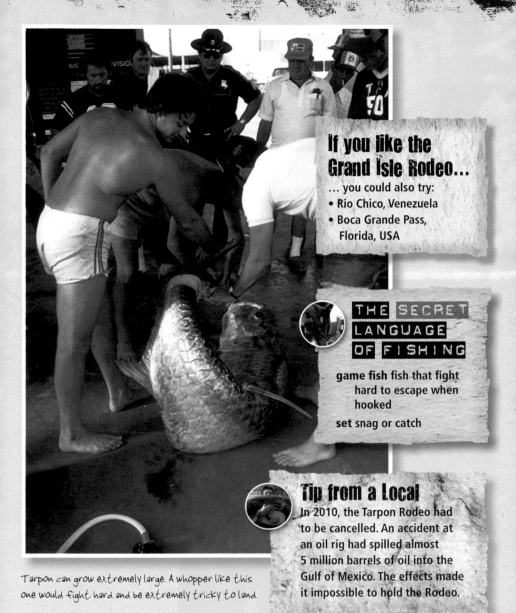

If you like the Grand Isle Rodeo...
... you could also try:
• Rio Chico, Venezuela
• Boca Grande Pass,
  Florida, USA

THE SECRET LANGUAGE OF FISHING

game fish fish that fight hard to escape when hooked

set snag or catch

Tip from a Local
In 2010, the Tarpon Rodeo had to be cancelled. An accident at an oil rig had spilled almost 5 million barrels of oil into the Gulf of Mexico. The effects made it impossible to hold the Rodeo.

Tarpon can grow extremely large. A whopper like this one would fight hard and be extremely tricky to land.

THE TARPON RODEO

The Tarpon Rodeo fishing starts at sunrise on Thursday morning, and the scales weighing fish close at 6 p.m. on Sunday. The big competition is for whoever can land the largest tarpon.

There's a big prize, too: in 2007, the winner got a new boat! There are also competitions for 27 other kinds of fish, including the famous, hard-fighting blue marlin, red snapper and speckled trout.

Sydney Harbour

Sydney Harbour is one of the world's most amazing places. The 244 kilometres (152 miles) of shoreline includes beautiful beaches, city-centre piers, steep cliffs, and wooded coast. The harbour offers pretty much every kind of fishing (apart from ice fishing!).

SYDNEY HARBOUR
Location: New South Wales, Australia
Type of fishing: sea (boat and shore)
Difficulty level: 2.5 of 5
Best season: all year round

Sydney Harbour's many wooden piers provide excellent fishing spots. You can drop your line straight into deep water, where the bigger fish are lurking.

Tip from a Local

The best time to fish is early in the morning, on a **turning tide**. Later on, boats criss-crossing the harbour will have scared the fish.

If you like Sydney Harbour...

... you could also try:
- Poole Harbour, England
- Halifax Harbour, Canada

Information: Extreme fishing

Many good fishing spots have become increasingly busy. This makes it harder to catch fish, and less peaceful. In response, some anglers have started fishing from hard-to-get-to places. This has become known as extreme fishing.

• Extreme fishing sometimes requires a long hike. For example, some trips to catch mahseer (see pages 26 and 27) require several days of walking and camping.

• Some anglers have started abseiling down cliffs to get to isolated fishing spots.

• In the 2000s, anglers in Australia and New Zealand started using high-speed jet skis and waverunners to race out to ocean fisheries. The craze soon began to spread around the world.

Each of these is extremely dangerous, and should only be attempted by expert anglers accompanied by a guide.

THE SECRET LANGUAGE OF FISHING

turning tide time when the tide changes direction

These anglers are perched on the edge of a seawater swimming pool at Avalon, north of Sydney. At least the barriers will give them something to hang on to if a wave tries to wash them away!

FISHING SYDNEY HARBOUR

It is possible to fish from the shore, but using a boat will make it easier to move on if the fish aren't biting. Look for quiet spots without too much boat traffic, where deep water becomes shallower. On any given day you might hook Australian bass, bream, kingfish, trevally, bonito, tuna – or even a marlin or a shark.

ESSENTIAL INFORMATION

The fishing is good in the harbour all year round. The size and number of fish you can keep is limited on some species: check **http://tinyurl.com/dcowg2** for more information.

Fishing equipment: A boat rod or a breakable spinning rod, depending on how you are fishing, plus a fixed-spool reel and a variety of baits and lures.

Clothing: The sun is always strong here, even on dull days, so cover up. A warm jacket can be useful, especially in the early morning or evening.

Mull

Mull is an angler's paradise. It is a beautiful, mist-shrouded island off the coast of Scotland. The rivers and **lochs** contain wild trout, and the deep seas off Mull are famous for producing some of the biggest fish ever caught in the UK.

Sea fishing off Mull

Much of Mull's coast is made up of high cliffs, so the best way to fish in the ocean is from a boat. In the Sound of Mull (between Mull and the mainland) some real giants are lurking. In 1986, the biggest skate ever caught in the UK was landed. It weighed 103 kilograms (226.6 pounds) – more than the man who caught it! The Sound is also a great place to fish for sea bass.

The steep cliffs of northern Mull allow anglers to try for deep-sea fish from land. They're no good if you're scared of heights, though!

MULL
Location: Western Isles, Scotland
Type of fishing: all kinds
Difficulty level: 2.5 of 5
Best season: May to October

If you like Mull...

... you could also try:
- Vancouver Island, Canada
- Cairns, Australia
- Kona, Hawaii, USA

THE SECRET LANGUAGE OF FISHING

loch Scottish lake

SKILL
Boat fishing

Fishing from a boat uses different techniques to fishing from shore. The rods are shorter and stronger – deep-sea fish may be heavy!

Tip from a Local
Mull was formed by a volcano. The volcanic rock means magnetic compasses often do not work in the area.

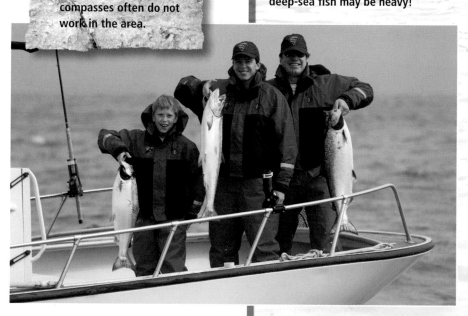

These guys have hooked some pretty big fish. Deep-sea fish are often larger and stronger than those found closer to shore.

ESSENTIAL INFORMATION
Scotland can be wet at any time of year, and in the winter it also gets cold and stormy. The most enjoyable times of year for fishing are probably spring and autumn.

Fishing equipment: Standard boat rod and a fixed-spool or special boat reel, plus tackle for whatever you're fishing for.

Clothing: Dress warm and dry, whatever the time of year.

1. Let your line go freely over the side of the boat. Just dangle it, there's no need to cast.

2. Wait until you feel the line go slack. This means the weight at the end has hit the bottom.

3. Reel in slightly, until you can feel the weight tugging on the line once more. Now let tiny bits of line out until you feel the weight resting on the bottom.

Set your hooks and bait as far up or down the line as you think the fish will be feeding. For bottom-feeders, for example, the hooks should be at the same height as the weight.

Ascension Bay

After a fishing trip to Mull (see pages 16 and 17), you'll probably need to warm up! Where better than the sunny, warm waters of Ascension Bay in Mexico? As well as having great weather, this is a place that has REALLY great fishing.

ASCENSION BAY
Location: Yucatan, Mexico
Type of fishing: sea (shallow water)
Difficulty level: 3 of 5
Best season: February to June

FISHING ASCENSCION BAY

The most popular type of fishing here is fly fishing. You can fish from a **skiff** or just by wading out into the shallow water. The Bay has many shallow **lagoons** where you can catch bonefish and tarpon. Both these fish fight hard when hooked, and are thought to be among the world's most exciting to catch.

A kayak is a great way to get around the shallow waters of Ascension Bay.

If you like Ascension Bay...

... you could also try:
- Lower Biscayne Bay, Florida, USA
- Rio Colorado, Costa Rica

Tip from a Local

If standing in the sea to fish, wear long, quick-drying trousers – they will protect you from stinging "water fleas".

SKILL
Fly casting

Look closely, and you can see the line looping forwards as it follows the tip of the rod. (This is equivalent to step 4 in the instructions below.)

ESSENTIAL INFORMATION

Fishing using nets is banned in Ascension Bay, which is partly why the waters are so teeming with fish.

Fishing equipment: A 2.75 to 3-metre (9 to 10-foot) fly rod with strong, heavy line to make casting easier on windy days.

Clothing: The sun is strong, so cover up with a hat and long sleeves/ trousers. Always wear eye protection when fly fishing.

THE SECRET LANGUAGE OF FISHING

skiff small, wide boat that can float in very shallow water

lagoon large area of shallow water

The best way to learn fly casting is in the middle of a big, grassy field, with no hook attached to the end of the line. It's safest for everyone!

1. Step backwards until about 5 metres (16 feet) of line is stretched out in front of you, with the rod tip on the ground.

2. Keeping your wrist rigid, lift the rod to about a 10 o'clock position (if seen from the side). The line should begin to lift smoothly off the ground.

3. Smoothly continue to accelerate the rod backwards, until it is at the 12 o'clock position. The line will start to snake through the air behind you.

4. When the weight of the line pulls the rod tip backwards, bring the rod forwards again. The line will follow back through the air and stretch out in front of you.

5. Stop the rod at about 10 o'clock, and let the line settle on the ground.

19

Door Peninsula

The Door Peninsula juts out into the waters of Lake Michigan. To the west is the strip of water known as Green Bay. The little creeks, inlets and bays on this side of the Door Peninsula are an excellent place to try catching one of North America's favourite fish – the smallmouth bass.

DOOR PENINSULA
Location: Wisconsin, USA
Type of fishing: lake (boat)
Difficulty level: 3 of 5
Best season: May and June

SMALLMOUTH BASS AND THE DOOR PENINSULA

Smallmouth bass are popular with anglers because when hooked, the fish fights hard against being landed. Some anglers say that for its weight it fights harder than any other fish. Some of the best smallmouth fishing is on the Green Bay coast near the town of Sturgeon Bay. There are also good spots between Egg Harbour and Fish Creek.

A smallmouth bass takes the lure. The angler on the boat is in for an exciting battle as he tries to land this fierce little fish.

Tip from a Local

If you're visiting in summer, bring some insect repellent – the mosquitoes can be vicious!

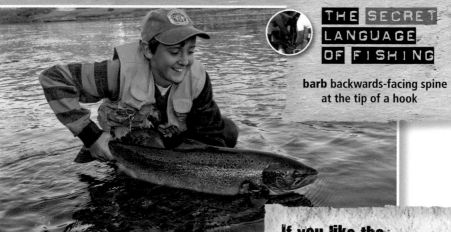

THE SECRET LANGUAGE OF FISHING

barb backwards-facing spine at the tip of a hook

Imagine catching a salmon as long as your arm! This boy is about to let his fish slip away, back into the water.

If you like the Door Peninsula...
... you could also try:
• Lake Powell, Utah/Arizona, USA
• French Creek, Pennsylvania, USA

SKILL
Catch-and-release fishing

Many anglers now use catch-and-release techniques, in an effort to make sure that fish numbers do not decline too much.

• Do not use hooks with **barbs**, as these damage a fish's mouth when it is being unhooked. Barbless hooks may even allow you to release a fish without removing it from the water.

• Land fish as quickly as possible. Otherwise, they may be so exhausted that they cannot swim away even after being released.

• Handle fish as little as possible in the dry air. Wiping the slime off a fish's scales with your hands is not good for its health.

• If the fish is tired, try "swimming" it back and forth in the water, while gently cradling it in your hand. This may give it enough oxygen to start moving again.

ESSENTIAL INFORMATION
Although it's possible to fish from the shore or by wading, the best way to fish off the Door Peninsula is probably by boat.
Fishing equipment: Smallmouth bass can be caught using fly, spinning or bait equipment.
Clothing: Dress for the season; if wading, a pair of warm waders will make the sometimes-chilly waters of Lake Michigan more comfortable.

Kristiinankaupunki

There can't be too many world-famous fishing spots where you have to wear a survival suit! The Gulf of Bothnia, between Finland and Sweden, is one of them – at least in winter. Here, the big attraction for anglers is the area's world-famous sea pike.

KRISTIINANKAUPUNKI
Location: Gulf of Bothnia, Finland
Type of fishing: sea (boat)
Difficulty level: 3.5 of 5
Best season: May, September to December

FISHING KRISTIINANKAUPUNKI

All kinds of fish swim in the icy waters of the Gulf, including whitefish, zander, grayling, salmon, sea trout and perch (which can be caught in winter through a hole drilled in the ice). But *you're* coming here to fly fish or spin for BIG pike – one of the meanest, toughest fish around. If you're lucky, you might hook one of 10 kilograms (22 pounds) or more.

Tip from a Local
This is one area where you'll definitely want to hire a local fishing guide – these waters are rocky and hazardous!

In winter, pike can be caught using nets dropped through holes in the ice.

trace length of wire or strong nylon leading from the end of the fishing line to the hook

SKILL
Playing a fish

If you like Kristiinankaupunki...

... you could also try:
• Prince William Sound, Alaska, USA
• Chiloé Island, Chile

This trout still has plenty of fight left, before it can be reeled in.

ESSENTIAL INFORMATION

The best time of year for pike fishing is in September and October, as the water begins to get colder.

Fishing equipment: For pike, the most important bit of kit is wire **traces**, as pike will bite through nylon. A rod and line strong enough to land a fish of 10 kilograms (22 pounds) or more is also required.

Clothing: Mosquitoes can be a problem in summer, so stay covered up. In winter, full survival gear is usually needed.

Hooking a fighting fish like a pike is only half the battle. The next steps are to play it and bring it in to the boat or shore.

1. If the fish races off, let out some line. If you try to stop it, the line will probably break.

2. As the fish veers left or right, start to reel it in. This will pull it steadily towards the boat (or bank).

3. As it gets close to you, the fish may race off again. Let it, then reel it in as in 2, above. The fish will soon get tired enough for you to pull it in close by.

4. Use a net or lip gripper to lift the fish out of the water, and then remove the hook.

23

The World's Biggest Fish

Some anglers aim to catch fish that put up a good fight. Others go fishing for food and try to catch fish that taste great. But there are a few anglers who just want to go large. In fact, they want to hook the biggest possible fish.

It's hard to tell which one looks more surprised: this 95-kilogram (209-pound) catfish or the man who caught it.

THE WORLD'S BIGGEST FISH
Location: worldwide
Type of fishing: all types
Difficulty level: 5 of 5
Best season: all year round

Tip from a Local

If you're fishing in the Mekong River, bring a strong rod – the river is home to more species of giant freshwater fish than anywhere else.

MEKONG GIANT CATFISH

In 2005, one lucky angler caught a very large Mekong giant catfish. In fact, it was the biggest **freshwater** fish ever caught, anywhere in the world. It weighed an incredible 293 kilograms (644.6 pounds). That's as much as a grizzly bear!